SYBLUES BOX OF

JAMAICAN RECIPES

SYBLUES
BOX OF
JAMAICAN RECIPES

Sybil Lewis

MOUNTAIN ARBOR PRESS

MOUNTAIN ARBOR
PRESS
Alpharetta, GA

ISBN: 978-1-63183-089-1

10 9 8 7 6 5 4 3 2   0 5 0 3 1 7

Printed in the United States of America

⊗This paper meets the requirements of ANSI/NISO Z39.48-1992 (Permanence of Paper)

Contents

Introduction

Sybil Antoinette Lewis is an icon in the restaurant landscape of Hartford, Connecticut, and Atlanta, Georgia. With her husband, Reynald Lewis, this dynamic duo has been the proprietors of a number of very successful restaurants for the past thirty-three years. Their first venture was the highly rated Pastry Dynamics and Tropical Cuisine in Hartford, Connecticut, which served as a meeting place for the local community.

They relocated to Atlanta, Georgia, and opened what was to become known as an experience in fine dining at the Pepper Pot Restaurant, located in midtown Atlanta, Georgia. They were featured in the *Atlanta Journal-Constitution*. Here, they transported their unique flair for their outstanding food and service to Hapeville, Georgia, coupled with highly sought-after specialties such as their wide selection of natural juices like Jamaican sorrel; ginger beer; Irish moss; exotic, tropical fruit punch; and much more, and have consistently earned five-star ratings on Yelp.

Sybil was born in Palm, Linstead, St. Catherine, Jamaica, West Indies, to a warm and vibrant Caribbean family consisting of her mother, father, thirteen siblings, and her second niece, Carline, with whom she was very close. All were raised on a farm, and together as children they enjoyed life in the Jamaican countryside, where Sybil started early honing her culinary skills by cooking "Dolly Pot," food for her dolls and pets and any imaginary life that would eat it. She began writing down her recipes and collecting them in her Syblues box, which traveled with her for these fifty years. She went to college and trained as a home-economics educator, where she was able to share her skills and technology and her passion for using farm-fresh produce—along with her ability to create an incredible assortment of sumptuous entrees, pastries, and desserts. She made her first now-famous wedding cake at age eighteen.

In 2015, upon the couple's request, she produced a replica of that first cake to celebrate their fiftieth anniversary. Sybil has established her reputation as one of the most sought-after creators of specialty cakes for all occasions and supplies customers worldwide.

Sybil has been married to Reynald for almost fifty years. They have three children—Somie, Maydene, and Titch—six grandchildren, and two great-grandchildren and counting.

This treasure trove of recipes is Sybil's gift to family, friends, fans, and future generations, that they may enjoy the richness of West Indian cuisine and develop their own expertise in preparing these dishes, desserts, and juices.

General Household Hints

1. Keep baking soda at dinner parties. If candle flame spills, throw baking soda over the flame.

2. If kids are hungry before dinner, give them a piece of apple or a small carrot.

3. Use a solution of baking soda or vinegar to wash your glassware. It will make it glisten.

4. If there is no window cleaner to clean your glass, use diluted vinegar or white rum.

5. If you have no common pins while hemming, use paper clips or curling pins.

6. If you feel like you want to throw up, dilute a tablespoon of white flour in a tablespoon of cold water and drink it—it will stop.

Appetizers

COCONUT CURLS

COCONUT CURLS

Ingredients:

1 lb. sifted flour (2 cups)
¼ tsp. salt
2 tbsps. margarine
¼ cup water
1½ tsps. baking powder
½ tsp. nutmeg
½ tsp. mixed spice
1 tsp. vanilla extract
1 tsp. almond extract

Method:

1. Slightly grease a baking tray.
2. Add all dry ingredients to sifted flour into a bowl and crumble margarine.
3. Make a well in the center of dry ingredients and add vanilla and almond extract to beaten egg and water.
4. Place dough in refrigerator for half an hour. Dredge flour on pastry board or countertop and roll out dough to ¼ inch thick.
5. Turn oven to 375°F.
6. With a sharp knife, cut long, finger-size, 4–6-inch strips. Use both hands and twist strips to look like curls.
7. Place on baking sheet and bake for 25–30 minutes. Cool and serve.

CORNISH PASTIES

Ingredients:

2 cups flour
1 tsp. thyme
1 egg (beaten)
½ cup margarine
3 cloves garlic
½ tsp. salt
1 stalk scallion
1 small onion

Method:

1. Add salt to flour, then crumble margarine into flour. Use a knife and mix dough with ¼ cup cold water and form into a dough and place in the refrigerator to set for half an hour.
2. Season ground meat with ½ tsp. salt, 3 cloves of fresh, crushed garlic, 1 tsp. thyme leaves, 1 stalk scallion, and 1 small onion, finely chopped.
3. Season and cook over low flame for 15–20 minutes, then cool.
4. Dredge pastry board or counter with flour. Roll out dough and use a juice glass to cut out small rings. Fill each with ground filling. Brush edge with beaten egg and seal, then brush on top and place on a greased baking tray.
5. Bake in a 375°F oven for 25–30 minutes.
6. Serve hot.

CODFISH BALLS

Ingredients:

½ lb. codfish
1 egg (beaten)
1 tbsp. butter
1 clove garlic (crushed)
½ cup potato (crushed)
1 tbsp. bread crumbs
¼ tsp. black pepper

Method:

1. Wash codfish and soak in lemon or vinegar water for 2–3 hours.
2. Peel, cook, and crush potatoes.
3. Cook codfish after soaking and shred.
4. Add the shredded codfish to the rest of ingredients and mix well.
5. Roll into balls and then into bread crumbs (lightly).
6. Fry in deep oil for a few minutes until golden brown.
7. Put ball on absorbent paper to extract excess oil.
8. Serve hot.

STAMP AND GO

STAMP AND GO

Ingredients:

1 cup flour
2 tbsps. tomatoes (chopped)
¼ cup unsalted flake fish
¼ cup cold water
1 egg (beaten)
½ tsp. baking powder
¼ tsp. thyme leaves
1 stalk scallion (finely chopped)

Method:

1. Mix all ingredients together in a bowl to a dropping consistency.
2. Pour cooking oil in frying pan to cover bottom. Heat oil at 350°F, then slightly lower flame.
3. Use a tablespoon and drop batter into heated oil.
4. Lightly brown on each side for 4–5 minutes.
5. Place on absorbent paper. Serve warm.

SOLOMON GUNDY

Ingredients:

½ lb. red herring (unsalted)
½ lb. shad or mackerel (unsalted)
1 onion (chopped)
2 tbsps. olive or coconut oil
2 stalks scallions (finely chopped)
¼ tsp. allspice or crushed pimento seed
1 tsp. black pepper

1 country pepper (finely chopped)
2 tbsps. vinegar

Method:

1. Place herring, mackerel, or shad in boiling water and boil for 5 minutes.
2. Extract as many bones as possible and shred finely.
3. Boil vinegar and pimento seed in a frying pan for 1 minute.
4. Put fish in a bowl and fold in peppers, scallions, and onions.
5. Remove pimento seeds from vinegar and pour over mixture.
6. Refrigerate. Serve on crackers.

Soups

PEPPER POT SOUP

Ingredients:

1 lb. salt beef
1½ lbs. yellow yam
½ lb. white yam
½ lb. coco
1 hot, Scotch bonnet pepper
2 sprigs thyme
½ cup spinach (chopped)

4 cloves garlic (crushed)
4 okras
1 cup coconut milk
3 stalks scallions
1 cup flour

Method:

1. Wash and cut beef into small pieces, salt (optional), and boil.
2. Wash and clean vegetables, chop, and add to meat.
3. When meat is almost tender, add coconut milk, diced yellow yam, white yam, and coco.
4. Add Scotch bonnet pepper, thyme, scallions, and crushed garlic.
5. Make a dough with the flour, then make little dumplings (spinners) and add to soup.
6. Cook for additional 10 minutes. Serve hot.

FISH SOUP

Ingredients:

1 lb. porgy fish
1 lb. doctorfish
2 qts. water
1 lemon
2 stalks scallions
½ doz. small green bananas
1 doz. pimento seeds, thyme,
salt, and Scotch bonnet pepper
to taste

Method:

1. Clean fish thoroughly and wash in lemon water.
2. Boil fish for about 20 minutes.
3. Remove fish from the pot and strain, then remove bones.
4. Peel green bananas and cut into 1½-inch slices, then add to broth.
5. Return deboned fish to pot, add pimento seeds, thyme, and scallions. Add pepper and salt to taste. Serve hot.

BEEF SOUP

Ingredients:

3 qts. water
¾ lb. pumpkin
2 turnips
1 parsnip
3 carrots
2 cups flour
1 lb. yellow yam
3 stalks scallion
2 lbs. soup meat

2 sprigs thyme
4 cloves garlic (crushed)
Black pepper and salt to taste

Method:

1. Put soup meat in a large pot and boil for 50 minutes to an hour.
2. Dice pumpkin and all other vegetables and add to pot and yellow yam.
3. Make dough to form dumplings and add to pot.
4. Add salt and seasoning to taste. Serve hot.

RED PEAS SOUP

With oxtail, cow foot, cowskin, or salt beef

Ingredients:

1 lb. oxtail
1 lb. cow foot
Cowskin (optional)
¾ lb. sweet potato
½ lb. coco
½ pt. coconut milk
3 stalks scallions
3 sprigs thyme

1 country pepper
1 big onion
1 lb. yellow yam
2 lb. flour
1 pt. red peas

Method:

1. Put red peas and meat to boil (wash first) in 3½ quarts of water.
2. When peas and meat almost cook, add coconut milk and ground provision and cook for about 15 minutes.
3. Make dough from flour, make dumplings, and add to soup with all seasoning. Add salt if needed.
4. Simmer for 10–15 minutes.
5. Serve warm.

Buns, Breads, and Puddings

BREAD-AND-BUTTER PUDDING

Ingredients:

8 slices bread
1½ pt. evaporated milk
½ cup currants or raisins (chopped)
1 tsp. almond
2 eggs
½ cup brown sugar
1 tbsp. butter
1 tsp. nutmeg
1 tsp. vanilla

Method:

1. Butter bread and cut into 2-inch squares.
2. Place bread and butter into a greased baking pan or pie dish alternately with currants or raisins. Put in layers.
3. Beat eggs, add milk and other ingredients.
4. Pour liquid over bread and sit for 1 hour.
5. Preheat oven to 375°F and bake about 40–50 minutes, or until top is golden brown.
6. Cool and serve.

BLUE DRAWERS OR SWEET POTATO DRAWERS

Ingredients:

2 cups cornmeal or 3 cups sweet
potato (grated)
1½ cups dark-brown sugar
½ cup raisins (chopped) (optional)
1 tsp. nutmeg
½ tsp. salt
1 tsp. vanilla extract
2 cups coconut milk

Method:

1. Mix all ingredients together and add a little water if needed.
2. Put on a pot of water to boil.
3. Drop or spoon ½ cup of batter on oiled banana leaves or foil.
4. Tie with cord or banana bark, put into boiling water, and boil for 1 hour or 1 hour 15 minutes. Lower flame.
5. When cooked, take out of boiling water. Cool and serve whole or sliced.

FESTIVAL

Ingredients:

2 cups flour
1 cup cornmeal
¼ tsp. salt
2 tsps. baking powder
½ cup of sugar
1 oz. margarine

Method:

1. Mix all ingredients together. Add water to form dough.
2. Put to set in the refrigerator. Cover with plastic wrap.
3. Heat oil in a frying pan at 325°F. Fry in deep oil to cover festival.
4. Roll in palm of hands lengthwise and timely put in hot oil.
5. Turn each festival until done. They must be light brown.
6. When done, place on absorbent paper to extract excess fat.

CHRISTMAS PLUM PUDDING

CHRISTMAS PLUM PUDDING

Ingredients:

¼ cup white rum
1 lb. margarine
2 tbsps. butter
8 eggs
1 cup red wine or red label
3 cups all-purpose flour
2 tsps. baking powder
⅓ cup burnt sugar

½ tsp. ground cinnamon
1 tbsp. molasses
1 tbsp. honey
1½ cups sugar

Fruits (chopped) are subject to soak in red wine and Jamaican white rum for weeks or months before using.

Method:

1. Cream butter and margarine with sugar until lightly fluffy.
2. Add eggs two at a time and continue to beat.
3. Pour in burnt sugar and stir.
4. Add all the rest of ingredients except flour and dry spice.
5. Sift flour, baking powder, and dry spice.
6. Cut and fold flour alternately with wine to make a batter.
7. Hold up batter in spoon at 45° angle. Batter must have a dropping consistency back in the bowl.
8. Use a rubber spatula to clean batter from bowl, then pour into a greased baking pan and put in a preheated oven at 300°F for 2–2 ½ hours.
9. Cover baking pan with foil, place in another pan of water before steaming.
10. When baking, insert a skewer in center.

JAMAICAN SWEET POTATO PUDDING

JAMAICAN SWEET POTATO PUDDING

Ingredients:

2½ cups sweet potato (grated)   1 tsp. vanilla extract
½ cup flour   ¼ cup red wine (optional)
¼ tsp. baking powder   ½ cup raisins (chopped)
¼ tsp. salt   ½ cup evaporated milk
½ tsp. nutmeg   2 cups diluted coconut milk
½ tsp. allspice
¼ tsp. cinnamon
1 cup sugar
½ tsp. almond extract

Method:

1. Sweeten milk, and add spices and all ingredients together.
2. Pour mixture into a greased baking tin and cover with foil for the first hour.
3. Bake at 350–375°F for 1¾–2 hours.
4. Cool before serving.

CORNMEAL PUDDING OR PONE

CORNMEAL PUDDING OR PONE

Ingredients:

1 lb. cornmeal

¼ cup flour

1 tsp. almond

1 tsp. salt

3 cups coconut milk

¼ cup raisins

¼ cup currants

1 tsp. vanilla

1 tsp. mixed spice

1 tsp. nutmeg

1 cup sugar

1 qt. water

Method:

1. Sieve cornmeal and flour into a big bowl.
2. Add all ingredients and mix briskly until cornmeal and flour dissolve.
3. Pour into greased baking tin, cover with foil for the first hour.
4. Bake for 1½–2 hours at 375°F until top is golden brown and the middle is cooked.
5. Cool and serve warm or cold.

BULLAS

BULLAS

Ingredients:

2½ cups flour
1 tsp. baking power
¼ tsp. baking soda
¼ tsp. salt
½ tsp. vanilla
1 tsp. mixed spice
½ tsp. ground ginger
½ pt. dark-brown sugar
2 tbsps. melted butter

Method:

1. Use enough water to make sugar into a thick syrup.
2. Sieve all dry ingredients then make a well in the center and pour syrup in.
3. Add melted butter and vanilla and knead lightly.
4. Turn out on a floured board and roll out dough to a thickness of ¼ inch.
5. Use a pt. drinking glass to cut into circles. Carefully place them in a slightly greased baking sheet.
6. Bake in a preheated oven at 390°F for 20 minutes. Cool and serve.

EASTER HARD-DOUGH BUN

EASTER HARD-DOUGH BUN

Ingredients:

2½ lbs. bread flour
1½ lbs. chopped fruits of your
choice (namely prunes, raisins,
mixed peel, currants, and cherries)
3 tsps. rapid-rise instant dry yeast
1 tbsp. molasses
½ tsp. salt
1 egg (beaten)
1 pt. milk
1 tsp. nutmeg

½ lb. margarine
1½ cups dark-brown sugar
1 tbsp. burnt sugar
½ tsp. allspice
½ tsp cinnamon

Method:

1. Mix together flour, fruits, margarine, salt, dry spice, and sugar.
2. Dilute 2 tbsps. milk, then add 1 tbsp. sugar to dry yeast. Warm diluted milk and add to yeast in a small bowl and rub to a creamy paste.
3. Add ¼ cup milk to yeast and place in an area and let it sit there for a few minutes until it looks spongy.
4. Make a hole in the center of the yeast mixture and add beaten egg, molasses, burnt sugar, and milk and knead to a soft dough.
5. Cover and put in a warm area or on top of a pot of warm water, and dough will rise double in size, about 1–1½ hours.
6. Put dough on a floured board and knead, then put to rise again for another half an hour.
7. Knead again, then cut and shape in bun tin. Brush top with diluted milk and let it sit out for another 15 minutes.
8. Put into a preheated oven and bake for 1½ hours at 350°F.
9. Insert skewer in the center of bun. Skewer must come clean. Bun is done.
10. Slice bun when it is cool.

MOIST EASTER BUN

MOIST EASTER BUN

Ingredients:

2½ lbs. all-purpose flour

4 eggs (beaten)

1 bottle Guinness stout

1 bottle Malta

2 tbsps. honey

2 tbsps. molasses

½ cup evaporated milk

1 cup chopped, soaked fruits
(raisins, prunes, currants, cherries,
mix peel)

1½ cups sugar

1 tsp. vanilla extract

1 tsp. almond extract

½ lb. margarine

½ tsp. salt

1 tsp. nutmeg

1 tsp. cinnamon

1 tbsp. white rum

Method:

1. Crumble margarine into flour.
2. Add baking powder, salt, sugar, and dry spice. Mix in the fruits.
3. Make a well in the center and add all the rest of the ingredients.
4. Stir vigorously and give short strokes.
5. Pour into greased (lined) bun tins and bake in a preheated oven at 350°F for 2–2½ hours.

HOMEMADE BREAD

HOMEMADE BREAD

Ingredients:

2½ lbs. bread flour
1 stick margarine
½ tsp. salt
1 cup evaporated milk (diluted)
½ cup milk (warmed)
1 egg (optional)
2 tbsp. honey
4 tsps. dried yeast
2 tsps. sugar

Method:

1. Crumble margarine into flour, add salt.
2. Warm diluted milk and use 4 tsps. of the yeast and sugar and make a paste.
3. Add ½ cup warm milk to the paste and set aside in a warm area or close to flame until it forms a foam.
4. Make a well in the center of flour.
5. Add honey, beaten egg, and milk and mix to form a dough.
6. Put the dough in a warm area or on top of warm water. Leave dough in the bowl.
7. Let dough sit there to rise for about 1 hour. Double in size.
8. Knead dough on a floured board and put to rise again, 35–40 minutes.
9. Knead dough again, then cut and shape twists or fancy rolls.
10. Place on a lightly greased baking sheet and brush with milk or honey water.
11. Bake in a preheated oven for 50 minutes to an hour at 300°F. Time could be less or more depending on the size and shape of bread.
12. Insert skewer to make sure bread is baked.

Desserts and Icings

JAMAICAN RUM FRUIT CAKE

JAMAICAN RUM FRUIT CAKE

Ingredients:

1 lb. margarine	½ cup Jamaican white rum
2 tbsp. butter	1 cup red-label or port wine
8 eggs	1 tsp. vanilla extract
3 cups all-purpose flour	2 tsp. almond extract
3 tsps. baking powder	1 tsp. coconut flavoring
⅓ cup burnt sugar	1 tsp. allspice
1½ cups sugar	1 tsp. nutmeg
2 cups soaked fruits	

Soak fruits of your choice, like chopped cherries, prunes, raisins, and currants, for over a month in red-label or port wine, Jamaican white rum, cherry juice, and molasses (2 tbsps.).

Method:

1. Cream butter and margarine with sugar until lightly fluffy, then add 2 eggs alternately and continue to cream.
2. Pour in burnt sugar and soaked fruits.
3. Add white rum and timely mix in.
4. Add liquid flavoring.
5. Sieve flour, add baking powder, allspice, and nutmeg together.
6. Add flour to batter alternately with ½ cup of port wine and cut and fold until flour is dissolved.
7. Keep the ½ cup of wine until cake is baked. Batter must have a dropping consistency.
8. Pour batter into a greased and lined baking tin.
9. Bake in a preheated oven at 300°F for 1½–2 hours.
10. When done, insert a skewer in the center of cake. Skewer must come out clean.
11. When baked, sprinkle the ½ cup of wine over cake and leave to set for a few minutes.
12. Can be baked in round or oblong baking tin.

ROCK CAKE

Ingredients:

1½ cups flour
¼ tsp. salt
½ tsp. baking powder
1 egg (beaten)
¼ cup chopped raisins
1 tsp. vanilla
2½ oz. dark-brown sugar
2 oz. margarine

1 cup milk
½ tsp. mixed spice

Coconut flakes can be used instead of raisins, just to improvise.

Method:

1. Rub in margarine in flour with fingers until it looks like bread crumbs.
2. Add sugar, flour, baking powder, raisins, mixed spice, and vanilla.
3. Add egg and milk and mix well with a fork for a lightly stiff dough.
4. Spoon and form a rough heap and place on a greased baking tray.
5. Decorate on top of each rock cake with ½ cherry. Rake on each cake with a fork to give a rocky look.
6. Bake in a preheated oven at 400°F for 20 minutes.

ROYAL ICING

Ingredients:

4 lbs. confectionary sugar
½ cup shortening
2 tbsps. lemon juice
¼ tsp. salt
1 tsp. almond
2 egg whites (beaten)
¼–½ cup cold water
1 tbsp. white rum

1 tbsp. meringue powder can be used instead of the egg white.

Method:

1. Blend confectionary sugar 2 cups at a time with all the rest of ingredients until smooth.
2. Consistency should be firm and semisoft.
3. If icing is too stiff, add 1 tsp of water.

BUTTERCREAM ICING

Ingredients:

4 lbs. confectionary sugar
2 cups shortening
1 tsp. vanilla
¼ tsp. salt
¾ cup cold water

Cream cheese can be used instead of shortening.

Method:

1. Blend confectionary sugar 2 cups at a time.
2. Add the rest of ingredients and blend to a soft consistency or until peaks are formed.

Side Dishes

YELLOW YAM CASSEROLE

Ingredients:

2 lbs. yellow yam
½ cup flaked fish (deboned) (optional)
3 stalks scallion
2 tbsps. flour
2 tbsps. butter
1 tbsp. red bell peppers
1 tbsp. green bell peppers
1 clove garlic (crushed)

Method:

1. Peel, slice, and cook yam in a little salted water.
2. When cooked, crush coarsely in a big bowl and add butter, chopped scallions, red and green peppers, and garlic.
3. Cook and flake fish and add to the crushed yam.
4. Put 1 tbsp. butter in a saucepan and the 2 tbsps. flour to make a roux.
5. Rub constantly until flour dissolves.
6. Add ½–1 cup of water and season to taste.
7. Some chopped scallions can be added to the panada (sauce).
8. Grease a casserole dish and put the seasoned, crushed yam alternately with the sauce in layers.
9. Sprinkle paprika on top and bake in a preheated oven at 400°F for 20–25 minutes.

WHITE OR NEGRO YAM SALAD

Ingredients:

2 lbs. yam
2 tbsps. onion (grated)
3–4 stalks scallion
Salt and black pepper to taste
½ cup tomatoes (finely chopped)
1 tbsp. mayonnaise

Method:

1. Slice and cook yam in a little salted water and put to cool. Dice yam finely.
2. Combine the rest of ingredients and leave 1 tbsp. of chopped scallions for garnishing.
3. Fold salad a few times, then put in a serving dish over a bed of lettuce garnished with chopped scallions.
4. Keep chilled in the refrigerator.

RICE AND PEAS (RED BEANS)

RICE AND PEAS (RED BEANS)

Ingredients:

1 cup red peas
2½ cups rice
2 cups coconut milk
1 tsp. salt (or salt to taste)
2 stalks scallion
2 sprigs thyme
1 Scotch bonnet pepper
3 cloves garlic (crushed)

Method:

1. Put peas to boil into 1 quart of water until tender.
2. Add coconut milk and other seasoning and boil for about 10 minutes.
3. Add rice and briskly stir with fork.
4. Lower flame and let it simmer until water dries out.
5. Serve hot.

Hot Pepper Sauces

MANGO CHUTNEY

Mango Chutney

Ingredients:

2–3 half-ripe mangoes
3 cloves garlic
½ bell pepper
1 chocho (peeled and diced)
2 big Scotch bonnet peppers
¼ cup raisins
¼ cup currants
1 tbsp. almonds (crushed)
¾ cup dark-brown sugar

¼–½ cups apple cider vinegar
Pinch of salt

Method:

1. Cut hot and bell peppers and discard all seeds. Chop into small pieces.
2. Peel mangoes, discard seeds, and cut into chunks.
3. Wash and peel chocho, remove the heart, and dice.
4. Put all the ingredients together and pass through a mincer, or blend coarsely.
5. Boil over low flame until chutney begins to thicken.
6. Cook for about 25–30 minutes.
7. Cool, bottle, and store.

HOT PEPPER SAUCE

HOT PEPPER SAUCE

Ingredients:

1 doz. large Scotch bonnet peppers
(can be mixed)
½ cup carrots (boiled)
1 onion
2 stalks scallion
½ cup tomato
½ cup apple cider vinegar
½ cup water
½ tsp. salt
1 tsp. horseradish
½ tsp. mustard
¼ tsp. cream of tartar (optional)

Method:

1. Wash peppers and take out stems.
2. In a blender, put hot peppers and the rest of ingredients and blend until smooth.
3. Bottle and store.

Hot Cereals

GREEN PLANTAIN PORRIDGE

Ingredients:

1 big green plantain (grated or
blended)
½ cup evaporated milk
1 qt. water
1 tsp. vanilla extract
½ tsp. nutmeg
½ tsp. salt
1½ tbsps. flour
Sugar to taste

Method:

1. Peel green plantain.
2. Grate or blend.
3. Cook in 1 qt. of boiling water about 10–15 minutes, stirring constantly.
4. Add a little water to flour to make a paste, then add to porridge.
5. Cook for a few more minutes.
6. Sweeten to taste. Serve hot.

HOMINY PORRIDGE

Ingredients:

2 cups hominy corn
1 cup coconut milk
1 stick cinnamon
Sugar to taste
2½ tbsps. flour
½ tsp. nutmeg
1 tsp. vanilla
½–1 tsp. salt

Hominy corn can be soaked overnight for easy cooking.

Method:

1. Boil hominy corn in about 2 qts. water with cinnamon stick for an hour or until tender.
2. Add coconut juice.
3. Add a little water to flour to make a paste and add to porridge.
4. Add the rest of spice and sweeten to taste.
5. Serve hot and sprinkle a little nutmeg on top.

Beverages

RUM PUNCH

Ingredients:

½ cup lemon juice
2 cups white rum
½ cup grapefruit juice
1 cup strawberry syrup
¼ cup honey
½ tsp. nutmeg
¼ tsp. ground clove
¼ tsp. cream of tartar
1 drop angostura bitters

Method:

1. Mix all ingredients together in large bowl.
2. Bottle and chill.
3. Serve over cracked ice.

MATRIMONY

Ingredients:

1 custard apple
1 sweet sap
1–2 star apples
¼ cup condensed milk
½ tsp. nutmeg

Other fruit pulps can be used.

Method:

1. Wash fruits and remove seeds from pulps.
2. Mix all together with nutmeg and condensed milk.
3. Put in the refrigerator to chill for 25–30 minutes.
4. Serve cold.

GINGER BEER

GINGER BEER

Ingredients:

1 cup grated ginger
1 quart water
½ cup lime or lemon juice
½ cup honey
½–1 cup light-brown sugar
¼ cup pineapple (crushed)
(fresh pineapple)
¼ tsp. cream of tartar

Method:

1. Add to the quart of water ginger and pineapple.
2. Boil for about 10 minutes.
3. Put to cool and strain through a cheesecloth.
4. Add lemon juice, honey, sugar, and cream of tartar.
5. Mix well and put to chill.

Exotic, tropical Fruit Punch

EXOTIC, TROPICAL FRUIT PUNCH

Ingredients:

1 big mango (ripe)
1 cup watermelon (diced)
1 cup cantaloupe (diced)
1 cup pineapple chunks (fresh pineapple)
½ cup Otaheite apple (or regular)
¼ cup grapefruit juice
½ cup lemon or lime juice
¼ cup honey
¼–½ cup sugar
½ cup strawberry syrup

Method:

1. Blend all fruits to a smooth purée.
2. Add 1½–2 quarts of water and dilute purée (or to your consistency).
3. Add lemon or lime juice, grapefruit juice, honey, sugar, and strawberry syrup to punch and sweeten to taste.
4. Put to chill and serve over cracked ice.

SORREL DRINK

SORREL DRINK

Ingredients:

1½ cups dried sorrel
1 quart water
½ cup grated ginger
6 pimento grains
1 tsp. angostura bitters
¼ cup port wine
¼ cup white rum (optional)

One hundred percent grape juice can be used instead of port wine.

Method:

1. Put grated ginger in the pot with the quart of water and boil for 10 minutes.
2. Put dried sorrel in boiling ginger water.
3. Turn off flame and cover pot with a tightly fitted lid.
4. Leave to brew for 2–3 days.
5. Strain through a thick or double cheesecloth.
6. Add angostura bitters, port wine, and rum, and sweeten to taste.

BREADFRUIT PUNCH

Ingredients:

1 breadfruit
½ cup evaporated milk
¼ cup condensed milk
1 qt. water
1 cup sugar
¼ tsp. cream of tartar
½ tsp. nutmeg
½ tsp. salt
1 tsp. vanilla
1 tbsp. white rum
2 tbsps. port wine

Method:

1. Peel, slice, and boil breadfruit until tender.
2. Put to cool with breadfruit water.
3. Blend the breadfruit to a smooth consistency.
4. Add the rest of ingredients and blend for a minute.
5. Put to chill and then serve.

EGGNOG

Ingredients:

2 large eggs
1 tbsp. condensed milk
½ cup milk of your choice
3 tbsps. white rum
½ tsp. nutmeg
Pinch of salt
½ tsp. allspice
1 tsp. vanilla

Method:

1. Separate egg yolks from the whites.
2. Beat yolks until thick. Gradually add sugar and condensed milk.
3. Add egg whites and continue to beat.
4. Put mixture in blender and the rest of ingredients and blend for a minute.
5. Chill and serve. Sprinkle a little nutmeg on top before serving.

Liqueurs and Nonalcoholic Wines

Nonalcoholic Carrot Wine

Ingredients:

2 cups carrots (grated)
2 lbs. light-brown sugar
3 oranges
2 qts. water
2¼ tsps. dry yeast
6 cinnamon leaves
½ cup currants

Method:

1. Boil carrots and cinnamon in water.
2. Squeeze mixture through strainer.
3. Dissolve yeast and sugar in the mixture.
4. Juice oranges and add to mixture with ground currants.
5. Mix all ingredients together and set aside in a glass jar at room temperature for 27 days.
6. Filter through calico or flannel, and store. Wine tastes better when aged.

NONALCOHOLIC ORANGE WINE

Ingredients:

2 doz. oranges
1 quart water
4 cups brown sugar
¾ cup raisins
2½ tsps. dry yeast
1½ tsps. nutmeg

Method:

1. Boil water. Wash, peel, and slice oranges.
2. Pour boiling water over oranges and allow to cool.
3. Add the yeast and let it stand for 30 minutes.
4. Add sugar, raisins, and nutmeg.
5. Pour liquid in a glass jar and put in a cool place (do not refrigerate).
6. Let it sit for 14 days, stirring every other day.
7. Strain through calico or flannel.
8. Bottle and store.

PINEAPPLE LIQUEUR

Ingredients:

5 cups pineapple (finely chopped)
2½ cups lime juice
3¼ cups white rum
4½ cups brown sugar

Method:

1. Wash and finely chop pineapple (ripe).
2. Add to chopped pineapple lime juice and sugar. Mix well.
3. Tie thick cheesecloth or calico over deep pot.
4. Pour liquid in and let it drip overnight. Add white rum, and bottle.
5. Liquid must be clear (avoid sediment).
6. Put away at room temperature. Let it age for months and years.

Fish and Chicken

FRICASSEED CHICKEN

Ingredients:

1 4–5 lb. chicken, deskinned
and dejointed
½ Scotch bonnet pepper
3 onions
4 cloves garlic (crushed)
3 sprigs thyme
1 tbsp. tomato ketchup
1 tsp. browning
1 red bell pepper
1 green bell pepper
1 tbsp. seasoning salt
1 tbsp. all-purpose seasoning

3 tbsps. olive oil or coconut oil

3 stalks scallion
2–3 tbsps. bread crumbs
1 tbsp. butter or margarine

Method:

1. Deskin, dejoint, and wash chicken in vinegar water.
2. Drain well and season with sliced onions, chopped scallions, tomatoes, Scotch bonnet pepper, and the rest of ingredients (not the bread crumbs and oil).
3. Put to marinate in the refrigerator for about 2 hours.
4. Pour oil into cooking pot and heat at 350°F.
5. Dump everything in heated oil and cover pot and lower flame.
6. Stir occasionally. Pour 3–4 tbsps. water into pot and stir.
7. Cook for about 30–45 minutes.
8. Final 8 minutes in cooking, add 1 tbsp. butter or margarine, bread crumbs, 1 more sliced onion, and some chopped red and green bell peppers.
9. Serve hot.

Run Dung

Ingredients:

2 cups coconut milk
2 plummy tomatoes
1 small onion
1 Scotch bonnet pepper
2 stalks scallion
½ lb. unsalted shad, mackerel, or codfish
Salt to taste
2 sprigs thyme
2 cloves garlic (crushed)

Method:

1. Remove bones from unsalted fish and flake.
2. Put coconut milk to boil for about half an hour until you see a little oil almost formed.
3. Add flake fish to the pot, then season with the rest of seasoning.
4. Add a little annatto powder or curry for color. Finely chop all seasoning.
5. Simmer for 5–8 minutes and serve hot with your favorite staple.

ACKEE AND SALT FISH

ACKEE AND SALT FISH

Ingredients:

1 can or 2 cups cooked ackee
½ Scotch bonnet pepper
3 stalks scallions
1 tbsp. red bell pepper
1 tsp. black pepper
½ lb. unsalted codfish
2–3 tbsps. butter
2 tbsps. coconut oil

Method:

1. Drain ackee.
2. Boil unsalted codfish about 8–10 minutes.
3. Flake codfish in small pieces.
4. Sauté in butter and oil chopped scallions, red bell pepper, and Scotch bonnet pepper.
5. Add flaked codfish and stir.
6. Add ackee and sprinkle black pepper and swirl a few times.

Jerk Chicken

JERK CHICKEN

Ingredients:

1 4–5 lb. chicken
1 big onion
2 cloves garlic (crushed)
1 tsp. browning
1 tsp. allspice
1 tsp. black pepper
1 tbsp. dry jerk seasoning
¼ cup wet jerk seasoning

Method:

1. Cut chicken in four quarters.
2. Clean and wash chicken in vinegar or lemon water. Leave chicken skin on.
3. Dry chicken with paper towel.
4. Grate onion and garlic in a bowl and add the rest of seasoning and mix in well.
5. Place chicken quarter on a board and rub in seasoning thoroughly and put seasoning under the skin.
6. Put to marinate for 2 hours in the refrigerator.
7. Cook over open flames, grill, or in the oven.
8. If it is in the oven, place chicken on a baking sheet. Cover with foil for the first hour at 375°F (total 1½ hours).
9. Take foil off and cook for another 25–30 minutes until top is brown.
10. Put on a cutting board and chop into small and medium pieces.
11. Put chicken on a serving platter and pour the drippings from baking sheet over pieces of chicken.

ESCOVEITCHED FISH

ESCOVEITCHED FISH

Ingredients:

3 lbs. fish (whole or sliced) ½ cup water
1 tbsp. all-purpose seasoning 1 lemon
1 tsp. seasoning salt
1 or 2 Scotch bonnet peppers
2 large onions
3 tbsps. vinegar
1 tsp. allspice
1 cup cooking oil
1 tsp. black pepper
1 tsp. whole black-pepper grains

Method:

1. Clean fish thoroughly and wash in lemon water, then dry.
2. Slice if necessary.
3. Coat fish with dry seasoning and set aside.
4. Put fish in smoking-hot oil in a frying pan. Fry until both sides are crisp, and set aside.
5. Pour vinegar, sliced onions, pepper (cut up), and whole-grain black pepper into frying pan and bring to a boil.
6. When cool, pour over fish and leave to steep.

Curried Chicken

Ingredients:

- 4lbs Chicken
- 1 Medium onion
  - o Finely chopped
- 4 Stalks Scallions
  - o Finely Chopped
- 3 sprigs thyme or 1 tbsp thyme leaves
- 5 cloves crushed garlic

1 ½ tsps. Salt or to taste
½ tsp black pepper
2 tbsps blended fresh turmeric
or 2 tbsps ground turmeric
2 tbsps curry powder

Method:

1) Skinless, joint or cut chicken then wash
2) Put to drain, then place into large pan
3) Add all ingredients to chicken and rub in well
4) Cover tightly and put to marinate in refrigerator for two hours or overnight
5) Add 2 tbsps coconut or olive oil into a pot over flame. Heat until lightly brown
6) Pour everything into the pot and cover tightly, stirring occasionally and tip a little water each time
7) Lower flame and cook for 30 to 35 minutes
8) Serve over white rice or mashed potatoes

Beef

HOMEMADE BEEF PATTIES

HOMEMADE BEEF PATTIES

Ingredients:

Patty crust:
½ tsp. salt (½–¾ lbs. suet)
2 cups flour
¼ cup ice water
Yellow food coloring

Method:

1. Mix in flour, salt, and suet and a drop of yellow food coloring. Use ice water to make the dough. Make sure suet crumbles in the flour.
2. Wrap in parchment paper and put in the refrigerator until ready to use.

For the filling:

1 lb. ground beef	½ tsp. salt
½ Scotch bonnet pepper	1 tsp. paprika
3 sprigs thyme	2 tbsp. bread crumbs
3 stalks scallions (chopped)	1 tbsp. ketchup

Other ground meat, poultry, seafood, or vegetables can be used as filling.

Method:

1. Finely chop pepper and scallions and add to the rest of ingredients. Mix in with a fork.
2. Cook on top of stove for 20 minutes.
3. Roll out patty crust on a floured board. Use a dish to cut circles.
4. Put filling into each circle, fold, and seal.
5. Arrange in lightly greased baking sheet.
6. Put in preheated oven at 375°F and bake for 35–40 minutes. Patties look puffy when they are done.
7. Serve hot.

OXTAIL

OXTAIL

Ingredients:

3 lbs. trimmed oxtail
1 tbsp. seasoning salt
1 tbsp. all-purpose seasoning
1 tbsp. Worcestershire sauce
1 tbsp. browning
1 big onion (chopped or grated)
1 medium carrot (grated)
1 tbsp. bread crumbs
4 stalks scallions
½ tsp. black pepper

5 big cloves garlic
2 plummy tomatoes
1 cup flour (optional)
¼ cup lima beans
4 sprigs thyme

Method:

1. Wash oxtail and trim excess fat.
2. Add the ingredients except flour, lima beans, and bread crumbs.
3. Rub in thoroughly and put to marinate 4–5 hours in the refrigerator. Can be done overnight.
4. Put the seasoned oxtail in a tightly covered pot and put over low flame.
5. Let it cook for 1½–2 hours until oxtails are tender. Stir occasionally.
6. Knead flour in a tight dough and make little dumplings or spinners (optional).
7. Add dumplings, lima beans, and bread crumbs to cooked oxtails and simmer for 8–10 minutes.
8. Serve hot.

**POT ROAST JAMAICAN-STYLE
ROASTED BEEF**

POT ROAST JAMAICAN-STYLE ROASTED BEEF

Ingredients:

4–5 lbs. top or bottom round of beef
1–2 Scotch bonnet peppers
4 sprigs thyme leaves
1 tbsp. all-purpose seasoning
1 tbsp. seasoning salt
1 tsp. black pepper
6 stalks scallion
8 cloves garlic (crushed)
2 onions (finely chopped)

Method:

1. Wipe meat using vinegar or lemon juice.
2. Crush garlic and finely chop onions, scallions, and Scotch bonnet pepper.
3. Add the rest of ingredients and mix well.
4. Lay roast on a board and puncture a few holes all over with a sharp knife.
5. Rub roast thoroughly with the mixed seasoning and stuff into the punctured holes until seasoning is done.
6. Put in the refrigerator to marinate overnight, or 4–5 hours.
7. Tie roast with cord to keep punctured holes closed.
8. Put 1½–2 cups cooking oil in a Dutch pot to heat at 350°F.
9. Dust roast with flour all over to seal the holes.
10. Lower flame and put roast in pot.
11. Cover with a tightly fitted lid and cook for 1½–2 hours until tender. Turn roast occasionally.
12. Insert a skewer in center of roast. When skewer easily pulls out, roast is done.
13. Put on a cutting board and slice thinly across the grain with a sharp knife.
14. Serve warm or cold.

Vegetables

VEGETABLES COOK-UP

Ingredients:

1 medium carrot (diced)

1 cup cauliflower

1 cup broccoli

1 medium onion (finely chopped)

½ cup yellow squash (diced)

½ cup green squash (diced)

1 tsp. salt

3 cloves garlic (crushed)

¼ cup lima beans

1 plummy tomato

¼ cup red bell peppers

¼ cup green bell peppers

1 stalk scallion

1 tbsp. bread crumbs

2 tbsps. butter

Method:

1. Wash vegetables in slightly salted, cold water and put to drain.
2. Chop bell peppers, tomatoes, and scallions and add to the rest of ingredients.
3. Heat 2 tbsps. of butter in cooking pot, put everything in, cover, and cook until tender, about 10–12 minutes.
4. Serve hot.

STEAMED VEGETABLE MEDLEY

STEAMED VEGETABLE MEDLEY

Ingredients:

2 cups bok choy

¼ cup red bell peppers

¼ cup green bell peppers

¼ yellow squash

¼ cup green squash

¼ cup julienned carrots (peeled)

4–5 cups cabbage (shredded)

1 tbsp. sweet-and-sour sauce

1 tsp. salt

1 tbsp. butter or margarine

2 tbsps. onions (grated)

2 cloves garlic (crushed)

Method:

1. Wash and dry all vegetables.
2. Cut up bok choy, peppers, and squash into small pieces. Then mix in a big bowl with the other vegetables and cabbage.
3. Put vegetables into a big pot and add sweet-and-sour sauce, onion, and crushed garlic.
4. Put pot over flame uncovered and steam for about 8–10 minutes, stirring occasionally. A tablespoon of water can be added (optional). Vegetables contain water.
5. When done, vegetable medley must be crunchy and not soggy.
6. Scoop out of pot, preferably strained, and put into another container.
7. Mix in butter or margarine while hot and serve.

PHOTOS

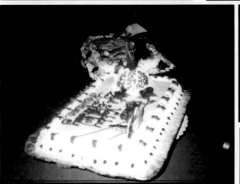

About the Author

Sybil Lewis has been married to Reynald, her teenage sweetheart and current business partner, for almost fifty years. She is a former educator with a passion for sharing her exemplary culinary skills with the young and young at heart. Her box is her gift to the future generation with the hope that it will encourage their skills to continue the tradition of fine West Indian cooking.